JUL -- 2013

Published in 2013 by The Rosen Publishing Group, Inc.
29 East 21st Street, New York, NY 10010

First Edition

Editor: Amelie von Zumbusch
Book Design: Liz Gloor and Colleen Bialecki

Photo Credits: Cover Sue Flood/The Image Bank/Getty Images; pp. 5, 7, 24 iStockphoto/Thinkstock; p. 9 Wild Arctic Pictures/Shutterstock.com; p. 11 Hal Brindley/Shutterstock.com; p. 13 Paul Souders/Stone/Getty Images; p. 15 Jupiterimages/Photos.com/Thinkstock; p. 17 Leonard Lee Rue III/Photo Researchers/Getty Images; p. 19 Gail Johnson/Shutterstock.com; p. 21 Paul Nicklen/National Geographic/Getty Images; p. 23 Rodney Ungwiluk, Jr. Photography/Flickr/Getty Images.

Library of Congress Cataloging-in-Publication Data

rumlin, Sam.
 alruses / by Sam Drumlin. — 1st ed.
  p. cm. — (Powerkids readers: sea friends)
  des index.
   978-1-4488-9642-4 (library binding) — ISBN 978-1-4488-9742-1 (pbk.) —
   78-1-4488-9743-8 (6-pack)
   s—Juvenile literature. I. Title.
   2D78 2013
   dc23

2012021116

n the United States of America

ation: Batch #W13PK3: For Further Information contact Rosen Publishing, New York, New York at 1-800-237-9932

PowerKiDS
Readers
SEA FRIENDS

WALRUSES

SAM DRUMLIN

PowerKiDS
press™

New York

D
W
Inclu
ISBN
ISBN 9
1. Walr
QL737.P
599.79'9-

Manufactured
CPSIA Compliance Inform

CONTENTS

Walruses are big!

They have fat called blubber.

It keeps them warm.

They live in big herds.

Clams are their top food.

Females are cows.

Males are bulls.

Bulls have longer **tusks**.

Most **calves** are born on the ice.

They grow fast.

WORDS TO KNOW

calf

clams

tusks

WEBSITES

Due to the changing nature of Internet links, PowerKids Press has developed an online list of websites related to the subject of this book. This site is updated regularly. Please use this link to access the list:
www.powerkidslinks.com/pkrsf/walrus/